Staying Safe at Home

This book is dedicated to safety in the home.

Staying Safe at Home

Donna Chaiet

THE ROSEN PUBLISHING GROUP, INC.
NEW YORK

The author makes no representations or warranties, actual or implied, as to the effectiveness or appropriateness of verbal or physical techniques because it is impossible to predict the variables in any given situation. The use of physical force in self-defense is a response option only when your life is in imminent danger and risk of physical injury is present. The laws regarding use of physical force in self-defense vary from locality to locality, state to state, and country to country, and the techniques described in this book may not conform to your locality's legal standard. In order to best learn and understand the techniques described in this book, "hands on" training and practice are necessary.

Published in 1995 by The Rosen Publishing Group, Inc.
29 East 21st Street, New York, NY 10010

Copyright 1995 by The Rosen Publishing Group, Inc.

First Edition

Manufactured in the United States of America.

Library of Congress Cataloging-in-Publication Data
Chaiet, Donna.
    Staying safe at home / Donna Chaiet.
      p. cm. — (The get prepared library of violence prevention for young women)
    Includes bibliographical references and index.
    Summary: Uses real-life examples to illustrate practical tips on how to avoid becoming the victim of both property crimes, such as burglary, and personal crimes, such as sexual assault, while in your own home.
    ISBN 0-8239-1863-7
    1. Young women—Crimes against—Prevention—Juvenile literature. 2. Violent crimes—Prevention—Juvenile literature. 3. Dwellings—Security measures—Juvenile literature. 4. Self-defense for women—Juvenile literature. [1. Teenage girls—Crimes against. 2. Crime Chaiet, Donna. Get prepared library of violence prevention for young women.
HV6250.4.W65C52   1995
613.6′0835′2—dc20   95-8492
                                                 CIP
                                                 AC

Contents

Introduction

This book addresses the types of situations you may encounter in or near your home that compromise your physical or emotional safety.

The goal of this book is not to frighten you or make you uncomfortable in your home. The goal is to make you aware of the types of crimes that occur in or near the home: property crimes such as burglary, and personal crimes such as sexual assault. The more information we have, the better able we are to address the situation. Therefore, this book suggests prevention techniques and solutions for situations in which prevention was not enough.

Personal safety in the home goes beyond what many people think of as home-safety issues, such as accidentally cutting yourself with a knife.

Discussing the home as a place unsafe for teens is not easy. To a certain extent we all live with an "illusion of safety" about our environment. Even though the media continually discuss violence, crime, weapons, and gangs, we believe those problems exist in other communities. If we really took the time to think about the level of violence in our neighborhoods, we might not be able to go to sleep at night. For some of you who live in neighborhoods marked by persistent violence, that may already be your way of life. For those who live in less obviously violent neighborhoods, it is hard to comprehend that you are vulerable.

Unfortunately, no matter where you live the potential exists for violence, both in stranger crime and acquaintance crime. Fortunately, with some education and training, you can learn to be self-reliant and take care of your personal safety. Just as you can learn what to do in case of a fire at home, you can learn to handle other potentially dangerous situations.◆

One of the ways a criminal can break into a home is through an unlocked door or window.

chapter 1

Home Safety: Property Crime

Essentially, a person has two reasons to want to break into your home. The first is to steal valuable property such as electronic equipment, jewelry, or cash. The second is to cause physical harm to someone in the house. It is possible that the person committing this type of crime, the perpetrator, is known to you, but this chapter focuses on crime committed by someone you do not know.

A stranger gains entry to your home by two basic ways. The first is by breaking in or taking advantage of unlocked windows or doors. The second way is to be invited in. How could that happen?

In his book *Street Sense*, Louis Mizell discusses the numerous guises that criminals may use to gain access to your home: faking their identity and pretending to be postal workers, maintenance workers, or ordinary people asking to use the phone.

Have you ever admitted a stranger because he wore a uniform? Or because he looked as if he needed help? Don't be fooled, especially if you are home alone. Ask that identification be slid under the door. Ask for the number of the main office and confirm that the person was assigned the visit. If you still don't feel secure, call a friend or neighbor to come over, or tell the visitor to come back when an adult is home.

Lara

Lara came home from school one afternoon and saw a van parked in front of her house. The van door was marked All-County Cleaning Service. A man and a woman approached her and said that her mother had arranged for them to clean the house. Lara remembered that her mom's back was bothering her, and she knew that relatives were expected in the next week. Her mom had never used this service before, but Lara thought maybe this time she had decided to hire someone to help her out.

Lara let them into the house and they began to clean. Half an hour later the woman said that they needed to get more supplies. They left and never returned. When Lara's parents got home that evening, she told them what had happened. Her mother said she had not called any cleaning service and checked her jewelry box. Everything was gone.

What could Lara have done? First, she should not have let anyone into the house whom she did not know. She could have checked out their story by calling her mother or father at work. She could have called the All-County Cleaning Service Office to see if it was legitimate. Many con artists work in male/female teams to help them gain access. Don't be deceived.

Toni

Toni was home alone one Saturday after-

You take safety precautions, like wearing your handbag strap across your shoulder, when you go outside. You need to take some precautions at home too.

noon. She lives in a rural town where the houses are far apart from each other. A stranger knocked on her door. Toni knew not to open the door. She asked what he wanted. He said his car had broken down and he wanted to use the phone. Toni said she would call the police department and have them send help. He then asked if he could use the bathroom. Toni really wanted to help this man out, but she decided to give directions to the nearest store that had a public restroom.

Toni made a lot of good decisions. Con artists often capitalize on the fact that people are generally good and helpful, particularly teenage girls. They understand that you want to be nice and help them out. Therefore, they frequently fake a need for assistance: a need to use the phone, or help in carrying packages because they have a broken arm. This doesn't mean that you should never help people in need. You *can* help in ways that don't compromise your own safety. So, assess your safety first, then be creative. In a situation like Toni's,

It s a good idea to study your home environment. You might check
out whether your neighborhood has a regular police patrol.

you could provide assistance in a number of ways. You can direct them to the nearest police station or gas station. You can make a phone call for help for them while they wait outside. You can call a trusted adult who lives close by. Most of you have a family rule about not opening the door for strangers. Now you know the reason for this rule. Follow it.

Finally, be careful if you have put an ad in a local newspaper to sell something or to run a garage sale. Make sure you are not alone when people come to shop. Place the merchandise outside or near the entrance so you don't have to bring someone through your house. (The same goes for answering an ad; go with somebody to look at the merchandise.)

Break-Ins

The above examples focused on efforts to gain entry to your home by using a con or a guise. What are some things you can do to prevent the likelihood of your home's being broken into?

The first thing you can do is examine

your home environment. Where do you live? Is it a house or an apartment building? If it is a house, how many floors are there? Is there a basement or an attic? If you live in an apartment building, what floor are you on? Is there a fire escape? Are there gates on the windows? Is there a doorman or a security guard? Knowing your environment and being aware of what resources are available to you is good personal safety.

Do a safety check of your home. Do all the windows lock? Do you keep them locked? What about the front door and back door? Is there an entrance via a fire escape or basement door? What kind of locks do they have? Who has the key? Are there bushes, an alley, or a vestibule where someone could easily hide? Is the area around your home well lit or is it dark? If you do not have locks on your windows, get them. Make sure that bushes are trimmed so that no one could hide there.

Be careful to whom you give a spare key and where you hide one. Under the front or back doormat, in the mailbox, or on the top of the door frame are obvious choices. Se-

It is good idea to choose a safe haven, such as a bathroom, and to have a portable phone available should your home be broken into while you are there.

lect a less likely spot, and change it frequently. Another safety tip that is inexpensive and easy to do is putting a deadbolt on the doors. You can use wood blocks shaped like triangles that fit under the door on the inside and make it difficult to open even if the lock is picked or broken. Home alarms are widely sold. Some of the newer alarms rely on changes in air pressure; if someone opens a door or window, the alarm goes off. More expensive systems include cameras, panic buttons, and sophisticated technology. These need to be installed by a professional. An easy thing to do is to drill holes into your window frames and put a nail through them to prevent the window from being opened from the outside any farther than the nail.

Finally, choose a room in your home to be a safe haven. A bathroom or small office would work. If possible, have a portable phone available so that you can call 911 even if the phone lines have been cut. The safe haven should have a second exit, such as a window or fire escape, so that you can get to safety. Install a deadbolt on the inside of this door, or have one of the door stoppers described earlier. This is to be a room to run to if there are burglars in the house. Call 911; identify yourself and where you are calling from, and tell them that your house has been broken into and a crime is in progress.

If you do not have time to hide or if you are surprised, do not get into a fight with the intruders. Make it clear that they can take whatever they want. Most of the property can be replaced; your life cannot.♦

chapter 2

Stalkers/Peeping Toms

*a*nother kind of criminal altogether are the stalker and the peeping Tom. A stalker is a person who repeatedly follows a victim over a period of time with the intent to instill fear or do physical harm. Famous people are often victims of this type of crime. John Lennon's murder, Teresa Saldana's stabbing, and the invasion of David Letterman's home are examples.

Recent attention, however, has been focused on noncelebrity stalking. An article entitled "Stalking—Chances are it could happen to you or someone you know" (*For Women First*, March 28, 1994) discussed average women who were being stalked. It pointed out that people have many different reasons for stalking, but the most common is being jilted in love. The situation becomes dangerous when the stalking or contact becomes persistent, harassing, and is accompanied by violent threats.

This type of crime is included in a home safety book because it is possible that you may be followed home or watched in or near your home.

Libby

Libby works at a local fast-food restaurant. A lot of the customers are regulars, and she jokes around with them. One of them, Marvin, recently asked her out on a date, and Libby agreed. Marvin asked her out again, but this time Libby politely declined. She liked Marvin but really wasn't interested in dating him again.

She noticed a couple of times last week that someone was following her home and to school. A friend told her that a guy had asked a lot of questions about her.

Libby became a little concerned. Why

A work environment can foster relationships that you don't want to carry over into your home environment.

was someone asking questions about her? What did he want? She continued to notice that someone seemed to be following her. She couldn't get a good look at him, but she thought he looked like Marvin. Then she received an unsigned letter in which the writer called her beautiful and asked to go out with her. What really scared Libby was that the writer said she should wear her red dress. Libby had just received a red dress as a gift from her aunt. She had unpacked it and hung it in her bedroom **23** *closet. The only way the writer could have seen it was if he had been in her bedroom or watching through her window.*

What should Libby do? Libby is being stalked, and she needs to contact the police. Awareness of this type of crime is slowly growing, and many states have enacted laws to help protect victims. The laws vary from state to state, and there is little precedent for how they can be used. Not many cases have been decided yet to guide lawyers, judges, and police. Libby should keep a diary of all of the times she thinks she is being followed and when friends and family have been questioned about her. She should save all the letters. She should not initiate any contact with the stalker at all.

If the police are unable to help her, Libby should change her schedule to make it more difficult for her stalker to know her whereabouts. She should become unpredictable about when she leaves the house, when she leaves school, and what her work schedule is. She should try to get

A self-defense class such as Prepare Self-Defense can teach you how to deal with many different types of assault.

people to escort her so she is alone as little as possible.

It is not a good strategy to ignore what is going on. Take every precaution. You are not being paranoid; you are being prepared. Consider taking a personal safety or self-defense class. The more prepared you are and the more information you have about this type of criminal, the better you will be able to handle any dangerous situation.

Another type of criminal who can threaten your home safety is a peeping Tom. This criminal is sometimes called a voyeur, someone who watches other people get undressed or engage in sexual activity. If you notice someone watching you from another building or from the street, close your blinds or draw the curtains. Call the police. Give them as complete a description of the person as possible. If you notice a pattern, keep a diary of when you are aware this is occurring. Again, pretending that it is not happening is not good safety.◆

chapter 3

Home Safety: People We Know

It is hard to believe that people we know would commit crimes against us. The murder of Nicole Simpson and the charges of O.J. Simpson's abuse of her during and after their marriage brought the issue of domestic violence to the public's attention. Domestic violence occurs in homes of all economic brackets, races, and religions and in rural, suburban, and urban families. A New York City Task Force on Family Violence reports that in 1992 there were 161,000 emergency calls to 911 reporting domestic violence. According to the U.S. Department of Justice report "Violence against Women," two thirds of all victims were related to or knew their attacker. Moreover, the report states that rapes committed by nonstrangers were more likely to occur at or near the victim's home (52 percent of the time).

Patricia

Patricia is 14 years old and lives with her mother. Her parents are divorced. Patricia's mother has a new boyfriend who stays over Friday and Saturday nights. Brian is generally pleasant and tries to be nice to her. He recently bought her ski equipment so that she could start skiing with the school club. The problem is that Brian sometimes makes Patricia feel a little uncomfortable. He looks at her in a sexual way and sometimes rubs up close to her.

One Saturday, Patricia's mother had to work. As Patricia was getting out of the shower, she noticed that the door was opened a bit and Brian was watching her. She shut the door, dried off, and thought that maybe she was being paranoid. A couple of weeks later he did the same thing, but this time he stood right in the open doorway. Patricia quickly grabbed a towel and told him to shut the door. Brian said that in his home people did not shut bathroom doors; that was their way of showing intimacy and affection. Patricia said that in her home the bathroom doors were shut and people did not see each other naked.

Patricia did not know what to do. Her mother really liked Brian, and except for these two incidents he did try to help her out. She decided that she would give Brian a break. Instead of telling her mother, she locked the bathroom door when she showered, figuring that would stop the problem. Unfortunately she was wrong. One morning, Brian slipped into Patricia's bed and started to stroke her body. He told her that she was beautiful, he really loved her mom and her and wanted to be part of their family. He took her hand and asked her to touch his genitals. Patricia pushed Brian out of her bed and firmly asked him to leave the room.

Sexual Assault

What happened to Patricia is called sexual assault. Sexual assault occurs when an adult engages you in sexual activity or touches your body in an overtly sexual way. Sexual activity includes sexual intercourse, touching of genitals, and oral sex. It doesn't matter whether the perpetrator uses violence or not; it is still sexual assault.

Sexual activity between people who are related by blood (a parent, sibling, cousin, or uncle) is called incest. Incest can also include any adult who lives in your home and engages you in sexual activity; this would include a mother's live-in boyfriend, a stepparent, or a stepsibling. Incest is sexual assault. Sexual assault is never the fault of the victim. Sexual assault is a crime.

What can Patricia do? The best way to stop incest is to talk about it. All states have laws mandating that certain professionals— school nurse, guidance counselor, police officer, or social worker—who know of incest in a home must report it.

If you believe that the parent who is not abusing you would listen to you and help you, then talk to that other parent. He or she may not have been aware of the prob-

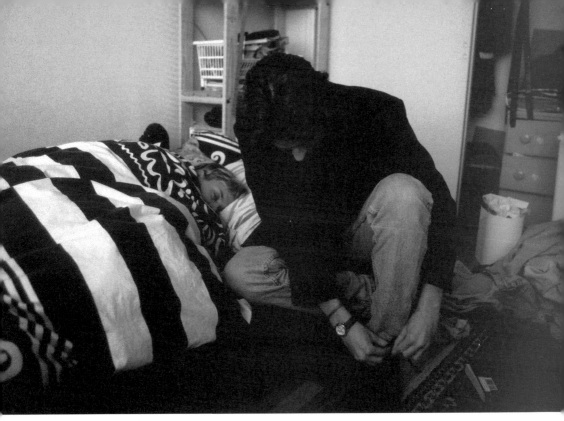

Consider talking to the nonabusive parent about what is happening.

lem and will take prompt action. It is possible that the nonabusive parent might end the relationship with the abuser.

Possible Strategies

Let's look at Patricia. She should address the problem as soon as possible. What strategy could she use for talking to her mother?

Step One: Get her mother's undivided attention. "Mom, I need to talk to you about something very important." Make sure she is actively listening.

Step Two: Lay out any ground rules for the talk. "What I have to say is really difficult for me to tell you, so I need for you to listen to me and let me finish before you ask any questions."

Step Three: Tell her exactly what happened. "About a month ago, Brian started watching me as I got out of the shower. I asked him to stop and he didn't. Yesterday morning he came into my bed and began to touch my body. He asked me to touch his penis. I told him to leave and he did."

Step Four: Ask for what you need. "I need for you to tell him to stop, and if he doesn't stop, I don't want him to spend time at the house."

Parents may have very different reactions. Be prepared for that. A person who came from a home in which abuse occurred felt powerless to change things then and may feel equally powerless now. Such a person may also believe that this is the way homes are. It is also possible that the parent is also being abused by the perpetrator and therefore feels at risk if she intervenes. She may be dependent financially and feel helpless to take any action. Or she may deny that there is a problem at all.

If the parent (or adult) you talk to can't or won't help, keep talking to other adults until you find one who will. Sometimes hearing this information is tremendously difficult for other adults, and the only way they can cope with it is to deny it.

If you are convinced that there is no way you can talk about what is happening, there are some things you can try to stay safe. Notice if there is any pattern to the incest/abuse. Try to alter your schedule to avoid being alone with that adult. This is not a foolproof system. The perpetrator will probably change his schedule or figure out a way to get access to you.

Another tactic is to confront the perpetrator. Tell him that if he does not stop you will report him to the police. This is a very difficult route to choose. First, it implies that you as the victim are responsible for stopping his behavior. You are *not* responsible for that. He chooses to victimize you.

Second, it might put you at physical risk. His behavior might become more violent. Proceed with caution.

Some of you who are experiencing incest at home may have been told that this is what families do. You may believe that the incest is your fault, that somehow you caused it. You may be afraid to tell your mother because you're afraid it will hurt her feelings. You may feel guilty or ashamed for not saying anything or for going along with it. You also may be scared. The perpetrator may have threatened you with harm if you told anyone. No matter what the case, incest and sexual abuse are not okay. They are crimes, and they are *never your fault.*

Seeking Help

This problem has no easy answers. The reasons for incest and sexual assault in families are many and complex. Many community organizations and school staffs are prepared to help you. Talk to a trusted adult and keep talking until you find someone who believes you and is willing to help you.

If the sexual assault is occurring with an

There are several people you can turn to if you are being sexually abused, including calling a hotline.

adult who is not a member of your household, such as a family friend, doctor, religious leader, tutor, or baby-sitter, you have more choices and options.

Many people believe that perpetrators are beasts who lurk in bushes. The reality is that sexual assault is more likely to occur with someone who is in a caretaking role with you. This person uses a pattern of behavior that coerces, manipulates, or tricks you into the sexual activity. Generally, he starts by winning your trust. He may **35** do this by offering you things you really want or by paying a lot of attention to you. Once he has your trust, he may very gradually begin to push your boundaries.

Boundaries are the physical space around our bodies. Most of you are aware of a certain bubble of space between you and another person that "feels right." This is sometimes called your "comfort zone." Comfort zones change from person to person and family to family. Some families hug and kiss each other frequently, and others rarely touch each other. The comfort zone can also change from situation to situation. How close do you get to a close friend? How close do you get to a new teacher?

One way that a perpetrator may push your boundaries is to stroke your hair or massage your back and neck. He may ask personal questions about your sexuality or what you like to do or what feels good to you. His behavior may then move into something more sexual like "accidentally" touching a breast or fondling your buttocks. It is possible that the attention feels good. You are an adolescent and have sexual

Your instincts will tell you when someone is invading your boundaries.

feelings. But that does not make his behavior okay; nor does it mean that you have consented to the behavior.

Be alert to this kind of conduct by adults who are in authority roles with you. It is not okay for someone to touch you without your permission. If he does, ask him to stop. Learning to identify your boundaries is difficult, and so is learning to enforce them. If someone's comments (emotional boundary violation) or the way he touches you (physical boundary violation) makes you feel uncomfortable, take note of it. You can enforce your boundaries by using a formula for easier communication. It is similar to the process described earlier:

Step One: Identify what you are feeling. "I feel uncomfortable."

Step Two: Say what behavior makes you uncomfortable. "When you touch my shoulders and give me a neck rub."

Step Three: Ask for what you want. "Please stop."

Practice enforcing boundaries in less

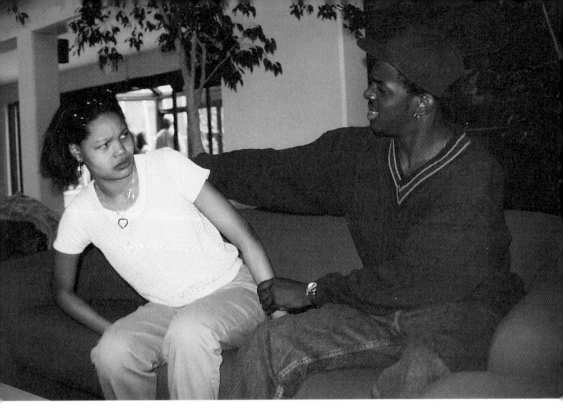

Don't be afraid to set your boundaries clearly by getting up and moving if someone sits too close to you.

emotionally charged situations. See how close you let people get to you before you are uncomfortable. See if you can ask someone who is crowding you to step back. Practice getting up from a park bench or school bus or train if someone sits down too close to you and there is room for the person to sit elsewhere. If you don't think you can do this or feel it is impolite, examine why you feel that way. Have you received messages that your feelings and wants are not to be respected? If so, examine what those messages were.

39

Young women are often socially conditioned that their physical and emotional boundaries are unimportant. Identify the messages that you have internalized. Ignoring your own feelings in order to protect or take care of someone else is potentially hazardous to your personal safety. Not asking a tutor to stop touching you during a private class may give him the impression that this behavior is okay. The sooner you say something, and the more decisively you say it, the more likely you are to stop the behavior before it gets dangerous or violent.

The above section discussed how you could try to prevent behavior that violated your boundaries. It should be clear, however, that it is not your responsibility to control adults' behavior. This book seeks to teach you skills so that you can become more self-reliant. However, the behavior may have reached the point where you need to get adult help. Maybe you have been threatened with violence, or you have asked him to stop and he won't. The best strategy is to tell a trusted adult.

Step One: Get the person's attention. "I have something important to tell you about my math tutor. I need your full attention."

Step Two: Lay down any ground rules. "I am not really sure what is happening, but it will help me tell you if you listen to everything I have to say before you react."

Step Three: Be specific about what has happened. If this person has access to your home (baby-sitter or tutor), be sure that he no longer does. "John, my math tutor, began touching my body during our sessions. I asked him to stop and he won't."

Step Four: Ask for what you want. "I don't want him tutoring me anymore."

You may want to report the incident to the police. Very often perpetrators have committed this crime with more than one person. Reporting is your choice; don't let anyone force you to do it. You also should know that if sexual intercourse occurred, you may need to get a full medical examination. You may be physically hurt, be pregnant or have a sexually transmitted disease. The earlier you know this information, the more choices you have on how to handle the situation.

The best way to handle sexual assault is to talk about it. Other options include avoidance tactics. For example, if it is a teacher or religious leader, do not meet with him alone anymore. If it is a baby-sitter or tutor, do not hire him. Avoidance strategies in this type of sexual assault may work better than with someone who lives with you. It is easier to avoid a teacher at school than a live-in boyfriend.

Verbal Boundaries

What happens if you find yourself alone with this person? You have already asked him to stop, and he did not listen. Be prepared to set very clear and direct verbal boundaries. For example, you might be doing homework in a library carrel. The math teacher stops and says, "I have missed our special sessions together. Why don't you schedule private tutoring this afternoon?" You could say clearly and loudly (remember it is a library; you may attract attention if you are loud, which is good): "Leave me alone. I don't want you to talk to me or touch me again." Pack up your books and leave. If this happens at home, you might consider threatening to report him or call 911. Often this kind of behavior succeeds because it is done in silence and secrecy. Once the behavior is publicized, it may stop. Use caution, however. This action can sometimes make the perpetrator more violent.

In addition to sexual assault, there is growing awareness of other problems that occur in the home to compromise teenagers' safety. Physical abuse, emotional abuse, and neglect occur in homes of all socioeconomic brackets. Like sexual violence, it is often difficult to address these problems because they go directly to the heart of beliefs about home life in the United States. For example, many households believe that physical violence is an acceptable (even desirable) form of punishment. "Spare the rod and spoil the

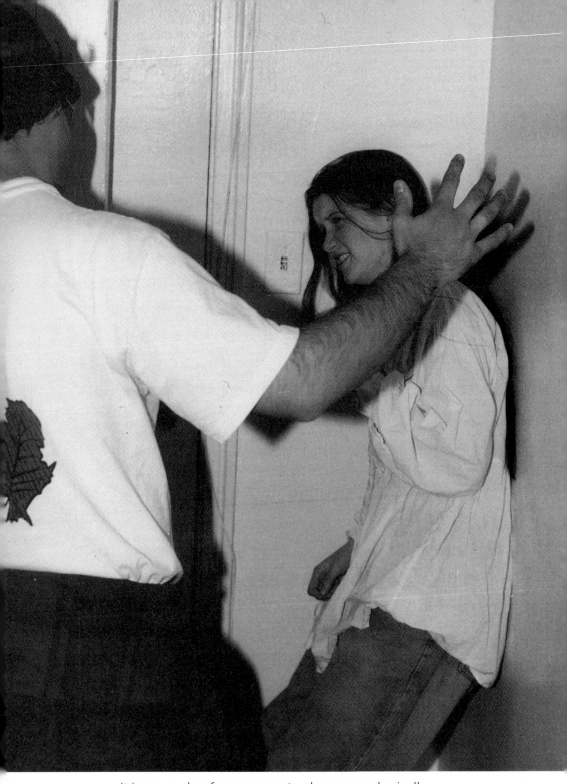

It is never okay for someone to abuse you physically.

child" is a sentiment held by many in the United States.

Current beliefs suggest that physical violence does nothing more than increase violence. An article entitled "But What About the Children?" (*The New York Times*, Section 13, August 14, 1994) reported that children who witness violence at home can confuse hitting with caring. Moreover, boys who grow up with violence are more likely to become abusers and girls more likely to become victims. If you are being beaten for no reason, the beatings are repetitive, you are hit in the face, thrown downstairs, or hit with an object, you are probably being physically abused. It is not okay, and the best way to handle this situation is to speak to a trusted adult.

What if you are not being hit, but there is never any food in your house or your parents leave you alone for long periods of time? This is called neglect, and it is even more difficult to define and address. An article, "Gang Girl—The Making of a Street Feminist" (*New York Times Magazine*, August 14 1994), described the home life of an urban girl named Tamika. Her mother is an alcoholic who does not work; her father sexually abused her and no longer lives with the family. Tamika is in charge of a gang begun by her boyfriend, currently serving time in jail. Tamika does not attend school regularly and is primarily cared for by a relative.

Tamika's story is shocking, but many girls are in similar situations. Unfortunately, there are no easy answers. The one ray of hope for Tamika is a community organizer who tries to provide an alternative to "street" life for the teens in her community. Reaching out to this person and talking about what is going on is the best way to deal with the overwhelming problems of family violence, abuse, and neglect.◆

chapter 4

Dealing with Stranger Violence at Home

This book has until now has emphasized being aware, being prepared, and telling a trusted adult as the best ways to handle potentially dangerous situations in or near your home. What if it becomes clear that the danger is based on hurting you physically (rape or murder)? What can you do then? Many law enforcement officials believe that the best way to survive an assault is to be passive. But new data indicate that forceful verbal resistance, physical resistance, and flight are behaviors associated with successful rape avoidance. Moreover, women who used forceful resistance were no more likely to be injured than women who did not resist.

47

Training in self-defense is a lifeskill that most young women (and men) can benefit from. In the self-defense classes in my course Prepare Self-Defense, students are taught skills (both verbal and physical) in realistic situations. The male instructors wear 40 pounds of padding so that students can practice techniques full force to the target areas of an attacker's body. These include the eyes, nose, temple, throat, groin, knees, shin, and instep. Additionally, students get to train in an adrenalized state. That is the body's mechanism to handle life or death situations. Sometimes called the "fight or flight" syndrome, it is a reaction in our bodies that prepares us to fight or run away.

Equally important to good technique is fighting spirit. In *Principles of Personal Defense*, safety expert Jeff Cooper describes seven principles of personal defense. Many have been described in this book already. They are **alertness, decisiveness, aggressiveness, speed, coolness, ruthlessness**, and **surprise**.

Jenny

Jenny was baby-sitting her younger sister

one afternoon. Hearing a rustling noise in the backyard, she went to check it out but saw nothing unusual. Then she heard glass breaking. Jenny was sure it was the back door. Her first instinct was to run out of the house; however, her sister was napping upstairs and she did not want to leave her alone. Jenny's family had a safety plan. There was a small bathroom upstairs with a deadbolt on the inside. Jenny ran to her sister's room, woke her up, and was about to head into the bathroom when she heard footsteps on the stairs. Jenny closed the door and tried to move furniture in front of it but couldn't. She picked up a lamp and waited, determined that when the door opened she would hit the intruder over the head. Fortunately, the burglar was interested only in property and did not check the other rooms. Jenny and her sister were not harmed.

What did Jenny do that worked? First, she was **alert**. She paid attention to subtle changes and trusted her instincts. Next, Jenny decided on a plan. The family had a good one, but because of circumstances

Be alert and listen to your instincts. If you feel uncomfortable, leave the scene.

she had to rethink a new one and did so **decisively**. Jenny got her sister and tried to move furniture in front of the door (**coolness**). When that did not work, she grabbed the lamp and decided what she would do (**aggressiveness** and **ruthlessness**). She planned to hide beside the door and hit the intruder over the head (**surprise**).

Deciding on the "right" decision in a dangerous situation is challenging. Whether you should run, hide, or fight back are all situation-dependent. The basis of good self-

There is no "right" decision in a dangerous situation. However, it does help to plan a next step if you are in such a situation.

Being prepared for potentially dangerous situations allows you to feel comfortable and confident at home.

defense is having many options and being able to think quickly and decisively. There is rarely one "right" thing to do. If you can't get away to safety (the very best option), doing something is usually better than doing nothing.◆

Conclusion

The first step in learning how to stay safe at home is to acknowledge that potentially dangerous situations occur in all settings. Start by taking an inventory of your home and see if there is anything you can do to make it safer. Check doors, windows, outside lights, locks, and shrubbery. Be prepared with a home safety plan. Check on strangers who want access to your home. Know that it is okay to ask an adult to come over or to make the repair person wait or come back when your parents are at home. If someone needs help, offer to call the police or direct them to **53**

Try to make your home as safe as possible by locking all doors and windows.

assistance such as a gas station or an all-night grocery.

If you are part of a family in which sexual assault or violence is occurring, speak about it to a trusted adult. If you are not believed, keep on talking about it until you find someone who believes you. You have a right to live free from sexual assault and physical violence. Community groups and governmental agencies are available to you. Look in the resource section at the back of this book for suggestions.

Know that fighting back in the face of a life-threatening situation is a choice. Take a self-defense class. Talk to your family about a safety plan, just as you would a fire drill. If you believe that your life is in immediate danger and you choose to fight back, go 100 percent—do not hold back. Be ruthless. Let your rage at what is happening fuel you to be powerful, strong, and decisive.◆

If you choose to fight your attacker, do so with all your strength
and concentration.

Glossary

acquaintance crime Criminal activity committed by someone the victim knows.

adrenalized state *See* fight/flight syndrome.

assailant Person who commits a crime.

boundary The physical distance or the emotional limit that surrounds a person.

boundary violation Event in which a person invades your comfort zone with either physical touching or verbal intimidation or disregard for your emotions.

comfort zone Your own personal physical boundary.

directive language Words that clearly state what you want: Stop, Back off, Go away.

domestic violence Form of violence that generally occurs in or near the home between a husband and wife, boyfriend and girlfriend, or parents and children.

fight/flight syndrome Biological response in which adrenaline and other hormones are released into the bloodstream, enabling the person to fight or run away.

illusion of safety Incorrect belief that an environment is safe in order to cope with a violent world.

incest Sexual activity between people who are related by blood.

perpetrator Person who commits a crime.

precedent Legal cases that have been decided and guide lawyers, judges, and police in handling new situations.

rape Forced sexual acts.

safe haven Room in your home designed to create safety during a potentially dangerous situation, such as a burglary.

sexual assault Criminal activity that includes sexual intercourse, touching of genitals, oral sex, or touching of the body in an overtly sexual way without permission.

societal conditioning The way in which society and the community affect the way you think and feel about yourself.

stalking Behavior in which a criminal follows his victim over a period of time with the intent to instill fear or to physically hurt that person.

stranger crime Criminal activity committed by someone the victim does not know.

violation Broadly defined, includes physical violence, sexual violence, property crime, sexual harassment, unwanted touching, and emotional abuse.

Resource List

General Information

Childhelp USA
6463 Independence Avenue
Woodland Hills, CA 91367
818-347-7280

National Coalition Against Domestic Violence
P.O. Box 18749
Denver, CO 80218
303-839-1852

National Committee for Prevention of Child
    Abuse
P.O. Box 2866
Chicago, IL 60690
312-663-3520

National Family Violence Helpline
800-222-2000

Institute for the Prevention of Child Abuse
25 Spadina Road
Toronto, Ontario M5R 2S9
416-921-3151

Information on Crime and Victimization

Crime Victims Counseling
P.O. Box 023003
Brooklyn, NY 11202-0060
718-875-5862

National Organization for Victim Assistance
1757 Park Road NW
Washington, DC 20010
800-879-6682

In Canada, call 1-800 VICTIMS (1-800-842-8467)

Rape Crisis Centers
(For a nationwide listing of rape crisis centers, call
    the Washington, DC, Rape Crisis Center
    Hotline, 202-333-7273, or check the phone
    book for local information)

Hospital Emergency Room
(Ask for Rape Trauma Center)

The Police
(for emergencies, dial 911; check the phone
    book for local information)

Ottawa Sexual Assault Support Centre Hotline
613-234-2266

Toronto Rape Crisis Centre Hotline
416-597-8808

Information on Self-Defense Training

Impact Personal Safety
19310 Ventura Boulevard
Tarzana, CA 91356
818-757-3963

Prepare Self-Defense
25 West 43rd Street
New York, NY 10036
800-442-7273

Woman's Way Self Defense
512 Silver Spring Avenue
Silver Spring, MD 20910

The YWCA and Martial Arts
(Check the phone book)

In Canada, call Impact Personal Safety at 818-
757-3963 for references to Canadian self-
defense programs

For Further Reading

Bass and Davis. *The Courage to Heal: A Guide for Women Survivors of Sexual Abuse.* New York: Harper Perennial, 1992.

Caignon and Groves. *Her Wits About Her.* New York: Harper and Row, 1987.

Cooper, Jeff. *Principles of Personal Defense.* Colorado: Paladin Press; 303-443-7250.

Kosof, Anna. *Incest.* New York: Franklin Watts, 1985.

Martin, Fay and Loreen. *No Is Not Enough.* San Luis Obispo, CA: Impact Publishers, 1984.

Spies, Karen Bornemann. *Everything You Need to Know about Incest.* New York: Rosen Publishing Group, 1992.

Index

Acknowledgements

This book is dedicated to Karen Chasen, the Executive Director at Prepare Self-Defense. Without her constant support, editorial eye, and sense of humor, none of these books would have been completed. Many other people have taught me about self-defense and personal safety. Listing them all would take many pages. However, my deepest thanks go to Lisa Gaeta, Director of Impact Personal Safety, Los Angeles. Lastly, I want to thank my parents, who have always taught me to "be aware."

About The Author

Donna Chaiet, a practicing attorney in New York City, is the founder and President of Prepare, Inc. Prepare conducts personal safety programs that teach teenagers the verbal and physical skills required to defend themselves by training them to fight against a padded mock assailant. Ms. Chaiet is a recognized speaker and conducts safety/communication seminars for schools, community organizations, and Fortune 500 companies throughout the United States. Ms. Chaiet's frequent television appearances include CBS, NBC, ABC, WOR, FOX, Lifetime, Fox Cable, and New York 1.

Photo Credits

Cover, pp. 2, 7, 9, 15, 18, 25, 35, 37, 50 by Michael Brandt; pp. 23, 31, 39 by Katherine Hsu; p. 44 by Marcus Shaffer; pp. 13, 51, 54 by Kim Sonsky, p. 52 by Yung-Hee Chia

Design

Kim Sonsky